Tracy L. Simmons 3/2/87

Purchased at Birds Etc #4.

Phx, AZ.

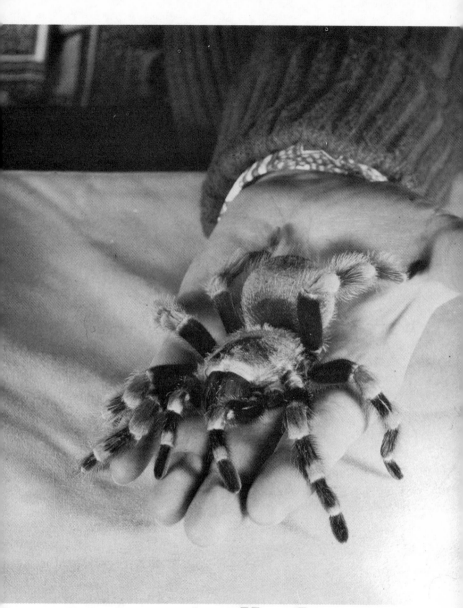

all about tarantulas
by dale lund

Cover photo by Dr. Herbert R. Axelrod.

Frontispiece by Dr. Herbert R. Axelrod.

All photos by Ken Lucas were taken at the Steinhart Aquarium, San Francisco, California.

Distributed in the U.S.A. by T.F.H. Publications, Inc., 211 West Sylvania Avenue, P.O. Box 27, Neptune City, N.J. 07753; in England by T.F.H. (Gt. Britain) Ltd., 13 Nutley Lane, Reigate, Surrey; in Canada to the book store and library trade by Clarke, Irwin & Company, Clarwin House, 791 St. Clair Avenue West, Toronto 10, Ontario; in Canada to the pet trade by Rolf C. Hagen Ltd., 3225 Sartelon Street, Montreal 382, Quebec; in Southeast Asia by Y.W. Ong, 9 Lorong 36 Geylang, Singapore 14; in Australia and the south Pacific by Pet Imports Pty. Ltd., P.O. Box 149, Brookvale 2100, N.S.W., Australia. Published by T.F.H. Publications, Inc. Ltd., The British Crown Colony of Hong Kong.

Contents

Dedication
To Alice Gray

ACKNOWLEDGMENTS

I wish to thank Mr. Bob Mackin of the Pets & Things pet shop, Lake Forest Park, Washington, and my wife Lilith for their help in the writing of this book. Special thanks go to Alice Gray of the American Museum of Natural History, whose patient correspondence kept alive my interest in the study of the remarkable tarantula.

The Tarantula as a Pet

If someone had told me when I was a child that in the future I would keep tarantulas for pets and even write a book on these "hideous" spiders, a cold chill would have crept from my nervous stomach slowly up my spine. And when it bubbled into the nape of my neck I would have given out a haughty laugh and told this foolish person that only a fool would do it. I was terrified of anything with more than four legs, and I proved it time and time again. Once, upon finding a

Considered by many to be unlovely to the point of being repulsive, tarantulas recently have gained a wider appreciation for their interesting habits and for their capacity to make long-lived and relatively undemanding pets. Photo by G. Marcuse.

Trying to protect themselves against what they mistakenly take to be the great danger posed to them by tarantulas, many people—young and old alike—will attempt to shield themselves against any tarantula they handle (assuming they can be coaxed into handling it at all) by wearing a protective garment such as the woolen glove used by this boy. Any wooly or otherwise loose-textured fabric, however, poses a danger to the tarantula, because the animal can get its appendages entangled in the fabric. Photo by Mike Huntington.

small, queer-looking spider on my arm while in school, I leapt to my feet, screaming and violently shaking off the intruder. The embarrassment resulting from the laughter of my classmates was not near as bad as having that atrocious creature on the bare skin of my arm.

And now I can admire the unique beauty of a tarantula in the palm of my hand. Thanks to the high school biology teacher who helped me acquire my first tarantula, I learned that one can indeed conquer his fears by confronting them. Nothing was more fearful to me than this largest type of spider known to man; and so, on a whim, I ordered one to see exactly what my demon was. To my surprise I found it to be a quaint little animal, as frightened of me as I was of it. Thus began an unusual friendship.

I still remember when I first watched this creature come walking out of the package, gracefully kicking her legs high into the air before she cautiously placed her feet onto the hard counter-top—350 million years of evolution stepping into my view. I did not know where to keep her or what to feed her; I knew nothing of a tarantula's lifestyle. After carefully prodding her into a jar, I immediately wrote to the American Museum of Natural History to see if someone there could help. Someone did, and my tarantula finally quenched her thirst, ate some food and moved into her new home.

Actually, there are few pets easier to care for than a tarantula. Feeding it once a week is sufficient; during the winter it may not want to eat at all. There should always be fresh water available. The spider's excretory product is a chalky substance which soon dries and disappears with no apparent odor. The cage needs to be cleaned only once a year, and even this is not critical. The spider carries no diseases as far as I know; a veterinarian is never needed. And if you decide to give it away or sell it, you should have little trouble finding a friend

One of the nicest features of keeping a tarantula as a pet is that it can be adequately and attractively housed at no great expense in either money or space to its owner. Photo by Dr. Herbert R. Axelrod.

who would enjoy adopting such a unique pet. I captured two large tarantulas on a highway in Texas and instantly found two friends at home who wanted them.

This spider is a conversation piece, to say the least. It's the first thing people want to see when they come to visit. I've loaned it to schools and have taken it with me to work. All people react differently, but all are fascinated.

If you are now the proud owner of a tarantula, I congratulate you on your wise choice of pet. You now have a book on its care—something I was never lucky enough to have. On the other hand, if you are trying to decide whether to get a pet spider, I hope this book will persuade you to do so.

What is a Tarantula?

To understand a tarantula in your home, it is best to understand it first in the wild. To begin, however, I will first introduce you to the confusion of the name "tarantula."

The spiders referred to in the United States as tarantulas are not really tarantulas at all, if by "tarantula" you mean the type of spider originally referred to as a tarantula. This was a European wolf spider, *Lycosa tarantula*, named after the town of Taranto in Italy. This species is a large and very hairy spider that digs a bur-

People usually think of spiders as the web-spinning creatures that we notice around our houses and gardens, but the class Arachnida, within which spiders and their allies are placed taxonomically, covers a very wide range of animals, including such diverse groups as scorpions, daddy longlegs and mites.
Photo by Muller-Schmida.

row, yet it is not so large as our native American tarantulas. The huge, primitive spiders that we call tarantulas belong to the family Theraphosidae of the suborder Mygalomorpha of the order Araneae (all spiders are included within the order Aranae). Europeans call them mygales or bird spiders, because some big, tree-dwelling species may capture baby birds in the nest. Possibly they were called tarantulas by the first Europeans to see them in the Americas because they are big, hairy and burrowing, like the native European wolf spider. To add to the confusion, *Tarantula* is the name of a genus of tailless whipscorpions, and to make matters even worse, *Mygale* is the generic name of a mammal—a water shrew! So you might try avoiding arguments pertaining to what your pet actually is on a taxonomic basis and just be content in calling it by its common name—tarantula.

These spiders are found in most tropical and subtropical regions of the world. In the Western Hemisphere they live mostly in tropical America, Mexico and the southwestern United States. You may see them on the open areas of a hillside, along the edges of cultivated land or in the sparse vegetation of a desert.

Some of the largest tarantulas are found in South America, such as *Lasiodora* of Brazil, with a body length of about three inches and a leg span of almost ten inches. Certain tropical species do not live in burrows but rather in silk tunnels constructed in trees. The United States alone has more than thirty known species, ranging in body length from 1.2 to 2.75 inches, with a leg span of about five inches. It is, however, almost impossible to tell many species apart without first killing them.

The spiders of the family Theraphosidae, which are commonly the ones sold in pet stores and to which this book is devoted, differ from other spiders in that

The spiders sold in the pet trade as tarantulas jibe in appearance with the popular conception of what a "tarantula" looks like—big, hairy, relatively heavy-legged spiders. Properly speaking, however, not all spiders that actually are tarantullas look like tarantulas, and not all spiders that look like tarantulas actually are tarantulas. The number of lungs possessed and the type of movement of the jaws are more important than size or hairiness in making the taxonomic determination of whether a spider is a "tarantula" or not. Shown here is a "typical tarantula" of the family Theraphosidae. Photo by G. Marcuse.

A view from below of the head of a theraphosid tarantula. The chelicerae move in a vertical rather than horizontal plane. Photo by Dr.
Herbert R. Axelrod.

they are among the largest, burrow rather than spin webs, have four lung slits instead of two, and have vertically moving fangs rather than horizontal-moving fangs. They are carnivorous, like all other spiders; they catch their prey with their jaws, inject it with venom, macerate the tissues and suck up the liquids. When mature, the males wander in search of a mate, but the females have been known to spend their whole lives within two feet of their first burrow. Tarantulas are nocturnal—active during the night and sluggish during the day. Where there is a cold season, they usually hibernate through the winter.

One of their most interesting natural enemies is the *Pepsis* wasp, or "tarantula hawk." Although this wasp is only one-tenth the spider's weight, it is a losing battle for the tarantula. A female wasp carrying a ripe egg will hunt from the air for the spider. Upon finding one, she will crawl under it and explore with her antennae to see if it is the correct species, since each species of wasp will kill only one species of tarantula. If the species is correct, she will dig a grave for it almost eight inches in depth, then return to thrust her body underneath the spider and plunge her stinger into a soft part. The tarantula will struggle hopelessly for a moment, then fall paralyzed. The wasp will then drag the spider into the grave, where she will lay the egg and fasten it to the spider's abdomen. The grave is then filled with soil which is tamped down (as best a wasp can tamp things down) so that the spot can no longer be identified. When the egg hatches in three days, the wasp larva eats the fresh body.

Although the *Pepsis* wasp is too fast for the tarantula to save itself, the spider does nevertheless have an instinctive alertness for this enemy. You can possibly test this on your pet. When a blunt object is pressed against its body, the spider will only walk away slowly. Yet if you hold an object above the spider, closely enough so that it can be detected, the creature will often raise itself on its hind legs and open its fangs.

Oftentimes I run into people who question the value of these peculiar spiders, so repelled by the animals' frightful appearance that they believe a wasp-dug grave is a good place for them. Tarantulas are the most primitive of the spiders, and if it were not for spiders, my belief is that we would not be alive today. They are effective allies in the war against bothersome and harmful insects, such as grasshoppers and locusts, that would destroy grain crops, and beetles and caterpillars that would consume green leaves. To give an idea of how many insects spiders consume, let us suppose that each spider eats a mere hundred insects during its lifetime (just two or three seasons for most species). The number of insects destroyed by spiders each year would outweigh the entire human race! Even if a female tarantula were to eat an average of only one harmful insect per week, by the time of her death she still would have made an impressive contribution to our war against insect pests. Tarantulas are helpful, not dangerous, to man, and should be appreciated.

The Anatomy

The spider's body is perhaps quite unfamiliar to you, and in having a tarantula it's handy to know the proper terminology for the parts of the body in case you are ever inspired to study your pet's biology, or if you ever have the opportunity to meet professionals in the field and talk with them about your spider. It's also nice to know the difference between the head and the tail; I've met more than one person who didn't.

The body has two main sections: the cephalo-thorax, which is the head and thorax combined, and the abdomen. The spider has no bones, but rather a tough skin that serves as an outer skeleton.

Some of the things that differentiate spiders from insects and other arthropods are well illustrated in this photo: spiders have four pairs of legs (the tarantula shown here is missing one leg), only two major body portions and no antennae or wings. Photo by Dr. Herbert R. Axelrod.

A tarantula's eyes, situated in a clump on top of the "head," aren't placed very efficiently by human standards, but tarantulas have gotten along with them very nicely supposedly a good deal longer than we have with ours. Photo by Muller-Schmida.

Eyes: Your pet has eight tiny eyes, clustered together in a bump on the carapace. There is some question as to how far the tarantula can see; however, it is no more than a few inches.

Mouth: The mouth is located on the underside of the cephalothorax, between and behind the chelicerae. It is easy to see, as it is surrounded by a reddish hue. Spiders don't chew their food, yet I have observed my tarantulas tearing down their food by manipulating their chelicerae.

Chelicerae: These are the two appendages located at the head, and are sometimes referred to as the jaws.

16

With these the spider seizes its prey. The poison glands are situated inside the chelicerae, and the fangs are situated at the ends. The tarantula may also use the chelicerae in digging its burrow.

Pedipalpi: These are the "auxiliary legs" in front of your pet's walking legs. The term means "foot-feelers," and that is precisely what they do. They serve as sense organs, not of touch alone, but of chemical perception as well. They are also used to manipulate the food. In males, the last segment is used in reproduction.

Legs: There are four pairs of legs, all attached to the cephalothorax. The little hole you see in the center of

This underside view of a tarantula distinctly shows the pedipalpi (the appendages closest to the head) and the spinnerets (at the other end of the tarantula, extending from the abdomen). Photo by Dr. Herbert R. Axelrod.

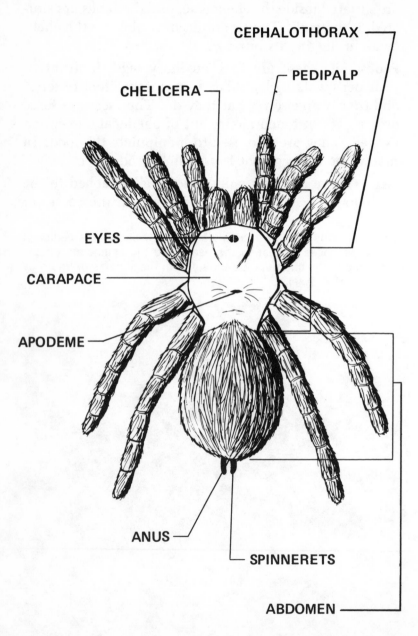

External anatomy of a tarantula as viewed from above.

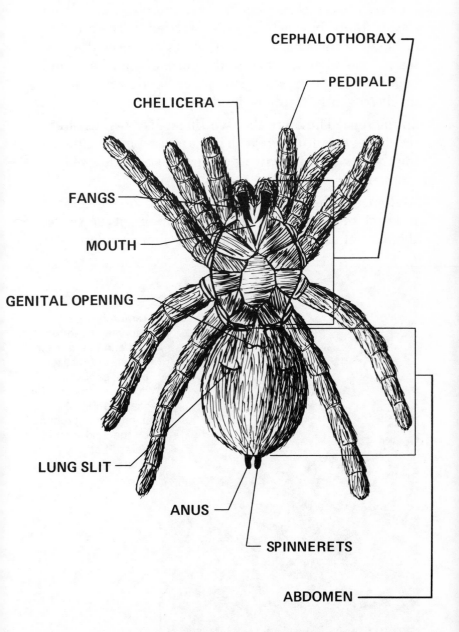

CEPHALOTHORAX

PEDIPALP

CHELICERA

FANGS

MOUTH

GENITAL OPENING

LUNG SLIT

ANUS

SPINNERETS

ABDOMEN

External anatomy of a tarantula as viewed from below.

the carapace is the "apodeme," the spot where the leg muscles are attached. Spiders have muscles which bend the leg joints, but their legs are extended by the pressure of blood in their bodies. Small claws are located at the feet; if you let your pet sit in the palm of your hand and begin to pick it up with your other hand, you will feel its claws gently trying to hold on.

Spinnerets: These are the two finger-like organs situated at the tarantula's rear. They are used in manipulating the silk as it is drawn out through countless microscopic tubes on the tips.

Abdomen: The abdomen contains most of the spider's internal organs. Silk glands take up a lot of space, though not as much as in more developed spiders. The

Tarantulas are capable of producing silk and using it for certain specialized purposes, but they don't use the silk for the creation of webs like the one produced by the spider shown here. Photo by Muller-Schmida.

reproductive, excretory, and respiratory systems are in the abdomen, and so are parts of the digestive and circulatory systems. On the bottom of the abdomen are genital openings and the lung slits through which the spider breathes.

Cephalothorax: This is the part of the body to which the legs are connected, and the part capped and protected by the hard carapace. It contains the spider's brain and central nervous system, and parts of the digestive and circulatory systems.

The hairs of the tarantula are highly sensitive, serving as organs of touch and possibly even organs of hearing and smell. Each hair contains a nerve that sends messages to the spider's brain, compensating for the poor eyesight.

It is still a mystery as to whether spiders can actually hear or smell. Some spiders, such as barking and whistling spiders in Australia and a purring spider on Staten Island, can make noises, so it is assumed they also might hear, but no one has found any ears. Also, if a female of certain species walks across a sheet of paper, a male will follow her trail accurately. Does this mean they can smell? No one knows for sure. They do, however, have a sense of taste, yet it's a mystery where it is located. Tarantulas will often discard acrid bugs such as certain beetles and cockroaches.

So although most parts of your pet have a name, much of its abilities are still a mystery. Perhaps you will discover some answers.

Selecting Your Spider

In choosing a tarantula, try to get a female. If only males are available, try to get an immature one. The reason for this is life expectancy: a mature male does not live more than a year at most after becoming adult, whereas the female may live ten to fifteen years longer. It takes either sex about ten or twelve years to grow up. If you are lucky enough to come by an immature female, you could very well enjoy her company through a graduation and a marriage and even have your children play with her when they are growing up. The tarantula has been referred to as the Methuselah of the spider world.

Before you purchase your pet, check under the knees of the front legs for small, thumb-like hooks. These are the sign of a mature male, and their presence is a sign that he will not live much longer. Adult males also tend to be lighter of body and have longer legs than females.

Most tarantulas offered for sale are males, since they are easier to catch. In the Southwest, just before the mating season, which occurs from September into October, swarms of males may be found wandering the countryside in search of mates. During this time they have been known to bite men or horses without provocation, yet they are usually quite slow and can be prodded into a container with little difficulty. The two that I captured on a highway in Texas could be seen from quite a distance as I drove up to them, and a ten-gallon water container and an empty dogfood box were perfectly suitable for transporting them home. Wandering males can even be spotted crossing roads during the night, casting huge shadows before the headlights of your car.

Mature male tarantulas have thumb-like hooks under the "knee" joints of the front legs; these hooks are used in mating. Immature and female tarantulas have no hooks. Photo by Ron Daniels.

Female and immature tarantulas, on the other hand, normally stay in their burrows and are difficult to capture. Coaxing one out requires imagination. Digging may injure the spider, and some burrows may extend several feet into the ground in several different directions. Flushing with water is a method often used, but this too may harm the spider—and it would require a lot of water.

An effective and humane method to seize a tarantula from its burrow is to "fish" for it. A piece of tough meat is tied securely at the end of a string and lowered into the opening. When it touches the burrow's first level it is jiggled to fool the spider into mistaking it for a live insect. When the spider grabs it, the string is slowly pulled. Now the tarantula may be fooled into thinking the bait is harmless food, but she will not be duped into letting the bait pull her out of the security of the burrow. To avoid having her let go when she comes to the entrance, the string is then jerked slightly, yanking the spider into the open. The burrow is then quickly covered so she will not return, and a good pet is captured.

The best species to choose is another matter. Pet shops may have nicknames for certain groups. An *Aphonopelma smithi* may be called a "Mexican brown," a *Dugesiella hentzi* may become a "Mexican red-leg," and so forth. Since identification of species is such a complicated question, these nicknames are a good idea. Most tarantulas make good pets, but a pet shop owner has warned me about two types that have given him trouble. One he calls the "Texas brown," or "cinnamon"—a general title for a brownish spider ranging from California through Texas. They have bitten him with little provocation. The other is the "black velvet," from Honduras. This spider ranges from Honduras up through western Texas, but only the southern ones are

There is not much difference between male and female tarantulas regarding their temperament and susceptibility to handling except that during the mating season males can be more irascible than they ordinarily are, and of course at such times they will be less amenable to handling. Females become more irascible when they are protecting their eggs. Photo by Dr. Herbert R. Axelrod.

especially bad-tempered. Perchance the pet shop owner's misfortunes were coincidental; possibly the spiders were males caught and sent to him during mating season. Nevertheless, he buys tarantulas by the hundreds, so it might be well to heed his advice. He recommends, among others, the Mexican red-leg, a larger tarantula whose legs sport reddish stripes, and the Mexican brown, which I purchased from him and have not regretted.

Of course, whether a tarantula is bad-tempered and may bite is a matter to be taken into consideration only if you wish to handle the spider. Many people keep this pet for many years without ever touching it. But if you want an animal that will be with you for a long time, get a female or an immature individual of either sex.

Housing

Tarantulas are escape artists. Unless the cage cover is fastened down in some way, the spider can line the wall with silk too fine for you to notice but strong enough to give the animal a firm foothold for lifting the lid. Once it was out, you'd be lucky if you ever saw your pet again. When I acquired my first spider, the high school also ordered one for the biology department. The biology department cage was made of flexible screen which finally gave way to the tarantula's pushing and pulling, and it was two months before they recovered the creature crawling from under a classroom heater, much to the dismay of a certain young lady.

There are several good vivariums, however, that you can buy. Most pet shops that sell tarantulas also sell suitable housing for them. One type comes in various sizes; it's made of clear plastic, with a removable top, and although it's intended for chameleons, turtles or plants, it is also suitable for tarantulas. If this terrarium is not available, one can easily be made from a fish tank having a secure cover.

The simplest and most inexpensive, although far from the best, vivarium is made from a gallon jar. The wide-mouthed kind is best because it's easier to get your hand out with the spider in or on it. Just cut out the middle of the lid with tin-snips and make a circle of screen to fit inside. The cardboard lining in the lid can be used as a pattern for the wire one. Be sure the lid can be screwed onto the jar. This cage can either stand on end or be made to lie on its side.

Fish tanks—the regular aquarium tanks sold in pet shops—probably are the best all-around tarantula domiciles available. In the first place, they come in a wide range of sizes, so you can get as elaborate and ambitious as you want to. You can set the size of the tank you buy according to how much money you care to spend. Some tarantula owners mistakenly get too large a tank, probably because they don't want to be stingy with the space they provide for a friend. In reality, the tarantula doesn't need a lot of room, so you don't have to go overboard on the size of the quarters you provide. A major advantage of fish tanks is that they are easily fitted with covers and lighting devices specially designed for them, so you don't have to dig up any makeshift covers (and since you *have* to have a cover, you might as well have one that fits well and looks good). Another point about fish tanks is that they provide a comforting feeling of security to people who otherwise might be a little edgy about viewing your tarantula. Guests expect captive animals to stay inside a nice roomy fish tank, whereas they might figure that a tarantula housed in an old pickle jar or shoebox or something could decide to crawl out—and onto their laps—at any time.

Your tarantula (unless it's a tree-dwelling species) will want to dig a burrow. If you give it enough earth, it will bury itself from view. If you want to prevent this, put a thin layer of sand in the bottom of the cage. If you want to see the burrowing, make the earth in the cage as deep as you can. By placing a smaller jar upside-down inside the gallon jar cage and covering it with earth, you can create an "ant farm" effect; the spider will have to make its burrow in the space between the two walls of glass where you can look into it. The tarantula may try to cover the glass; this can be prevented by putting a dark paper cover around the jar which can be removed for viewing.

The creation of an "ant-farm" effect is achieved much more easily through the use of fish tanks. You just take a fish tank and place it within a larger one, filling in the spaces between the glass with earth and presto!—

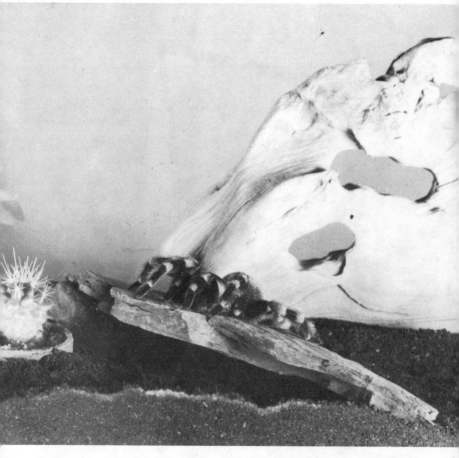

It takes very little work or expense to decorate an aquarium tank in a manner that makes the total effect safe for the tarantula and pleasing to the eye—the well-appointed tarantularium can add a nicely decorative touch to any room. Photo by Dr. Herbert R. Axelrod.

you have an instant viewing chamber, one that lets the tarantula burrow and dig and tunnel to its heart's content while allowing you to view all of the exciting activity. You can make your tank-within-a-tank tarantularium viewable from four sides or three sides or two sides, whichever you choose, depending on how you situate the smaller tank inside the larger one.

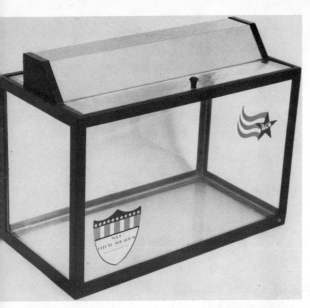

Fish tanks and related accessory pieces are ideally suited to use in housing tarantulas. The fish tanks themselves are relatively inexpensive and easy to keep clean, and they are easily made into escape-proof tarantula quarters through the use of covers designed for aquarium tanks. Most aquarium covers contain lighting units and therefore do double duty by providing both illumination and security. A special type of aquarium tank, designed for use with Siamese fighting fish (*Betta splendens*) provides a much lesser volume of space than other aquarium tanks but is compartmented and therefore allows the keeping of more than one tarantula in the same basic housing unit. Tank-dividers made for partitioning fish tanks can also be used to achieve the same effect.

Besides soil, other furnishings might include dry leaves, some dead bark and a few flat rocks, to give the spider places to hide. Depending on the space, a small piece of log having a wide crack or hole in it would be ideal. Once I even put two toys cars into my vivarium to see what the spider would do, if anything. Almost immediately she came over and stood on them, most likely out of curiosity as to what they were. But to my surprise, she then proceeded to bury them! Either she was hiding them for safekeeping or trying to do away with these intruders in her home; I never will know. Yet she spent hour after hour carefully placing the soil onto each exposed part of the two cars. You can try the same experiment with countless other objects.

The cage should be kept out of direct sunlight, which can make the inside of the cage hot enough to kill even a desert animal like the tarantula. The ideal temperature should remain at approximately 75°F. Under low temperatures the spider has been known to stop eating, and if it doesn't freeze to death it will starve to death. Growth of a young tarantula is so much affected by temperature that it may take one twenty years or more to mature in a cold climate. Our species can survive weather cold enough for snow to fall, but not for it to last more than a few days, and during this time the spiders are underground, where the temperature never drops to freezing. On the other hand, if the cage rises above 85°F, you will have trouble keeping water from evaporating too quickly, and your pet may die of thirst.

If you occasionally remove the remains of the spider's prey, you may never have to clean the cage further. Spider excrement is a thick, chalky fluid which soon dries with scarcely any odor; unless you look for it you may never notice it. In an earth-filled cage it just disappears. The spider doesn't mind it. However, if you do feel inclined to clean the cage, replacing the soil once

A tarantula's home need not be fancy. A few rocks placed so as to form a shelter, a few potted cactus plants or succulents and maybe a piece or two of driftwood are the only things required for simple tarantularium decoration—and those things are really more for the owner's benefit than for the tarantula's. Photo by Dr. Herbert R. Axelrod.

a year is sufficient. In my vivarium the glass tends to get dirty and has to be wiped clean about once a month.

Oftentimes the most exciting challenge in having a tarantula is to design its home. My brother and I constructed a large case for mine, made of wood with a heavy glass front, and containing a small light for heat and easy viewing. The floor is raised but drops down in front, creating the ant-farm effect. Its exterior is black and its interior is white, with a desert scene pasted on the back wall. My mother became so enthused with the

Steps in setting up a tarantularium that employs the tank-within-a-tank method to provide an ant-farm effect. At right are the two bare tanks, with the smaller placed inside and to one corner of the larger.

The filling operation has begun, with the soil (potting soil was used here) placed to cover one end of the smaller tank.

Photos by Dr. Herbert R. Axelrod.

The front half of the larger tank has now been filled with soil; height of the soil can vary according to the tastes of the owner but should not be greater than an inch or two below the rim of the lower tank, thereby preventing the tarantula from falling into the smaller tank and injuring itself.

project that she made a cloth cover for the case. Its furnishings include an odd piece of driftwood and a live cactus. This cage serves its purpose well, but I have yet to see anyone come up with a creative home that imitates the tarantula's natural habitat.

Many times the temptation has arisen to construct a giant facsimile of an ant farm, possibly even covering a small wall in my house, so the spider could have the freedom to dig tunnels where it will, and as deep as they are in the wild. All the twists, turns and side chambers would be open to view. The spider would set up its escape tunnels, leave the skins it had shed in side chambers and line all the walls with a fine layer of silk; the natural affairs of a tarantula, from eating to mating, could be observed day to day.

The "Habitrail" cage, available in most pet shops, may be worth trying out with a tarantula because of its infinite variety of tunnel layouts. The diameter of the tunnels, however, is intended for hamsters and is larger than the spider's average burrow.

WARNING: Never put two tarantulas in the same cage. They are cannibals. An exception to this rule, of course, occurs if you are attempting to breed them. See the chapter on breeding.

Feeding

If a tarantula is hungry, it will attempt to eat anything that is moving and smaller than itself. This includes other spiders, large insects such as crickets, grasshoppers, etc., small snakes, lizards, toads and baby mice. However, your spider can be tricked into eating even dogfood, which will be explained later.

Watching the spider catch its food is a fascinating experience; it's not often you will see it move so quickly. It may sit for days in the same spot, and suddenly, at the blink of an eye, pounce on a passing victim, grab it with the two chelicerae, and inject venom through the fangs to paralyze the prey. Then the spider usually remains still for possibly hours, manipulating and digesting its food. Often it will consume the entire carcass; sometimes, though, it consumes only the juices and leaves the carcass, which should then be removed.

One large insect a week is sufficient. The large Mexican red-leg and large tropical tarantulas may eat more. Ideally, all species should be fed every four or five days during spring, summer and fall. During the winter, where the weather is cold, the tarantula hibernates and may not eat at all, though it's a good idea to occasionally offer them food during this time. If the cage is kept at a low temperature, the spider will not eat and will eventually starve to death.

In proper conditions, a tarantula may be quite willing to eat a great amount of food. In two consecutive days I've watched the spider consume fifteen large crickets, five the first day and ten the following day. She would bite and paralyze one insect, drop it, spin silk around and around the body to prevent the possibility of its escape, and leave to kill another. She would then return, collect all the victims into one heap, and eat

Sometimes the tarantula can be coaxed into accepting a piece of soft meat dangled from a thread.

Opposite:
Prey's eye view of an advancing female tarantula.
Photo by Dr. Herbert R. Axelrod.

Housefly. Photo by Paul Imgrund.

Grasshopper. Photo by Muller-Schmida.

Cockroach. Photo by Paul Imgrund.

Hornworm. Photo by Paul Imgrund.

Scarabeid beetle. Photo by Paul Imgrund.

Insects and insect larvae are the natural foods of most tarantulas and are abundantly available most of the year. Certain insects and larvae, however, are rejected by tarantulas, and some (large beetles, for example) should be avoided because they pose a danger to the tarantula.

them. You cannot overfeed a tarantula. One will eat according to its hunger and ability.

If the temperature is kept at around 75°F in the cage and your spider has not eaten for awhile, yet it continues to refuse the food you give it, try changing its diet. Tarantulas do have a sense of taste. Some beetles and cockroaches defend themselves by giving off an offensive odor, and possibly they taste as bad. Your spider may attack an unpalatable insect but then back off and shake itself. There are few tarantulas, however, that do not enjoy crickets, grasshoppers and spiders.

If much time goes by and you cannot find a live morsel for your pet, don't worry. In laboratory tests, female tarantulas have been known to live more than

Mealworms (the larvae of a beetle, *Tenebrio*) are regularly stocked by many pet shops as live food for birds and reptiles and at some times of the year are the only live food you can obtain for your tarantula unless you raise your own. Shown here are adults, pupae and larvae of *Tenebrio*. Photo by Robert Gannon.

The hairiness of a tarantula's body and legs is well illustrated in this view of a tarantula's underside and the closeup on the opposite page. Some of the hairs serve as sensory instruments, and some are used in a peculiar defensive maneuver. Photos by Dr. Herbert R. Axelrod.

two years without food. You can feed your spider hamburger and even canned dogfood. This is done by compressing the meat into a small ball around the end of a piece of thread and jiggling it in front of the spider. When the animal grabs it, just continue to jiggle the thread gently until it slips out of the meat; the spider will think the "prey" is struggling to get away and will cling to it all the harder. This method provides the tarantula with food when live food is scarce, but when available I'm sure it would better appreciate something fresh.

You can also raise food. Often the spiders will eat mealworms, but they certainly enjoy crickets, which are a delight to keep. Some winged male crickets will lull you to sleep as they chirp softly into the night. You may wind up becoming attached to these little songsters and feel guilty feeding them to your tarantula, but this is nature's way. Your spider may eat the crickets, but your crickets would not hesitate to eat your carpet, clothing, linen, furs, paper, plants in your garden and even things made of rubber. They will also eat each other if they are hungry and together. If you live where these insects are abundant, you can find them in grassy areas or barnyards under boards or small piles of grass clippings. Sometimes you may find them in your own home. If they cannot be found, most pet shops that sell tarantulas or reptiles also sell crickets. The cricket cage should be ventilated by fine screen and furnished with a layer of dry sand (which should be changed occasionally), a place to hide and a roll of screening to be used for climbing and exercising. The entire cage should be kept in a dark place, and the temperature should range between 80° and 90°F. Do not put more than a dozen crickets in a three-gallon terrarium, and make sure you provide fresh food and drinking water at all times. They will eat lettuce, slices of apple, crushed dog biscuits,

Crickets, easily cultivated, are a mainstay tarantula food. Photo by Paul Imgrund.

flakes of uncooked oatmeal, peanut butter and cheese, and they should be given a variety of foods. If the cage is also provided with a bowl of sand which is always kept damp, the crickets will use this for egg-laying. If kept under the proper conditions, these insects will keep your tarantula healthy for as long as you wish to raise them.

An excellent book that provides directions to the raising of crickets, mealworms, roaches and a number of other insects is *The Encyclopedia of Live Foods*, by Charles O. Masters; the book is published by T.F.H. Publications and is available at pet shops and book stores. It deals primarily with the culturing of live foods for fishes, reptiles and amphibians but is of use to tarantula keepers because a number of these foods are also suitable for feeding to tarantulas.

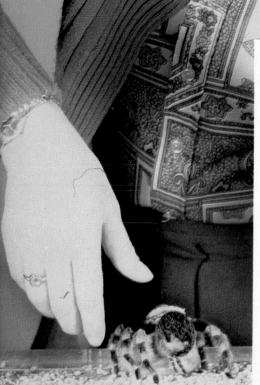

One good technique to use in picking up a tarantula is to quickly but gently insert thumb and forefinger on either side of the body between the second and third pairs of legs and lift up. Photo by Dr. Herbert R. Axelrod.

Opposite:
If carried in the open palm, your tarantula should not be lifted high, because if it were to fall it could easily be killed. Photo by Dr. Herbert R. Axelrod.

Water

In the wild the tarantula seldom gets a chance to drink and instead gets moisture from its food. In laboratory tests, female tarantulas have lived up to eighty days without water in the summer, and in the cooler seasons as long as seven months! Yet I have often watched them drink from a water dish, and it is recommended that while in captivity they should be provided with fresh water at all times.

Because its mouth is very awkwardly located for drinking from a dish, the spider must climb in to get the right angle. A heavy glass furniture caster makes an excellent water dish because it will not tip over. If a lighter dish is used, it should be pushed into the soil until the edge is even with the surface; otherwise the spider may upset it. In a pet shop I have seen them keep a small wet sponge in a dish, so the spider can drink much the same way it would drink from its food. If this method is used, the sponge should be moistened once a day, as the water would evaporate rapidly.

The Bite

All spiders are poisonous. Some can be deadly, such as the brown recluse and the notorious black widow, but not so with the tarantula. Although its bite can be as painful as a bee sting, it has never been known to be fatal to man.

The danger of the tarantula's bite is a superstition that dates back to the Dark Ages. Actually it was not our American tarantula at all that was the issue, but rather the wolf spider, *Lycosa tarantula*. During the Middle Ages in the town of Taranto, Italy, a curious outbreak of mass hysteria took place. People claiming to have been bitten by this spider were seized with a dancing frenzy, the idea being that the bite would be fatal if the victim did not dance hard and long enough to sweat the poison out of his system. The dance and the music to which it was performed were called "tarantellas" after the spider. This whole episode was a popular craze, not unlike "hula hoops," except that it involved a delusion—that the spiders bite people intentionally and that their venom is lethal to people. In truth, this European spider is no more venomous and no more prone to bite than the American wolf spiders, its relatives. (The wolf spiders (family Lycosidae), by the way, are *not* tarantulas.) No one knows for sure the reason for the supposed outbreak of biting and dancing. One theory is that the dances, which were community affairs rather than individual performances, were actually pagan religious festivals disguised as medical procedures to deceive the clergy.

The pain from the bite comes from the puncture wound of the fangs rather than from the toxin. The venom is comparatively mild, intended as it is to paralyze only animals smaller than the tarantula. Of course,

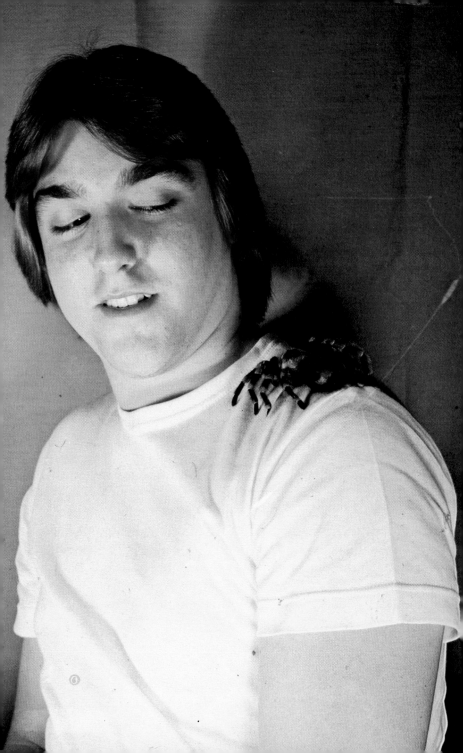

The photos on this page and opposite illustrate the type of playful but dangerous-to-the tarantula antics that some unthinking owners engage in after they have subdued their initial shyness at handling their pets. Were the tarantula to fall from either of the positions shown, it probably would be killed. Photos by Dr. Herbert R. Axelrod.

bee stings are not intended to kill people, either, but they do, and so do such relatively "harmless" stings as ant stings. Much depends on *your* biology, not the tarantula's. Therefore the best rule to adopt in handling tarantulas is this: when in doubt, don't.

What is more common is an allergy to tarantula hairs, which can cause a rash on some people. These hairs are often used by the spider as a defense mechanism. When irritated, tarantulas actually comb the hairs off their abdomens with their hind legs and throw them at the enemy. If flung into the nose or eyes of a lizard or mouse, they often divert the attack.

Captive tarantulas seldom try to bite. Toddlers play with them in tropical countries. However, if by some chance you are bitten, just treat the injury like any other puncture. At worst, it may make you sore and feverish for a few days, but it will do you no serious harm.. If you're one of the unlucky hypersensitives, you'll soon know it after you've been bitten, so get to a doctor as soon as you can.

Handling Your Spider

There are two ways to pick up a tarantula. One works because the spider is not aware that it is being picked up, the other because the spider has no way of preventing it. The first method is to put your hand down in front of the spider and then gently prod it from behind to make it walk onto your palm. The spider should sit there for as long as you want to hold it. Try not to let it get its claws into any rough material such as cloth. If this happens, you cannot make the tarantula let go without hurting it; you have to goad it gently into walking off of its own accord. The second method of handling the spider is to grasp it by the sides of the carapace between the bases of the middle pair of legs with your thumb and forefinger. Come down on the spider from above and pin it to the ground. It will probably crouch and sit still. When you are sure of your grip, pick up the spider quickly so that all eight legs lose contact with the ground at the same time. This is something that never happens in nature, so the animal has no way of acting under such circumstances. The result is that it doesn't act at all. It just freezes. This method can be used to look at the underside of your pet. Remember, however, that if even one foot touches anything, the spider will begin to struggle, trying to right itself and secure a firm foothold again.

If you are too apprehensive to be gentle and slow-moving in picking up your pet, it is best that you do not handle it. Nothing so alarms a spider as a sudden movement. And be very careful not to drop the animal. If it falls to the floor, its abdomen will burst like a paper bag full of jelly. Even the tree-dwelling species, which have been known to jump up to twenty feet, cannot stand a fall. Burrowing ones can jump up to six feet, yet I have

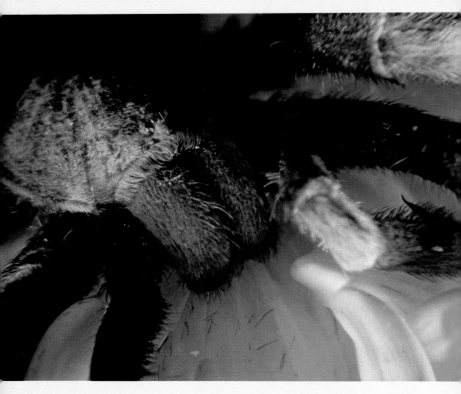

The eyes of this male tarantula, positioned midway between the chelicerae at the frontal edge of the carapace, are easily visible here. All tarantulas have eight eyes, arranged in a group. Photo by Dr. Herbert R. Axelrod.

Opposite:
The legs of a tarantula are somewhat fragile under conditions of captivity, but the loss of one or two legs is not overly serious. The animal still will be able to get around and will regenerate the legs during its next moult. This tarantula is missing one leg; the arrow points to the spot from which the leg has been broken off. Photo by Dr. Herbert R. Axelrod.

Gripped properly between the second and third pairs of legs, the tarantula's natural tendency is to extend its free legs and remain immobile. Photo by Ron Daniels.

An alternative method to picking up the spider from above is to nudge it gently onto your palm. Photo by Dale Lund.

not seen a captive tarantula, of any species, leap more than two inches. When the spider jumps of its own accord, it has the ability to land on its feet, but they don't have control in a fall, and it is fatal.

Because it is nocturnal, the tarantula is easier to handle during the day while it is sluggish. Also, the hotter it is, the more active the spider will be—and they can be quick.

It may be possible to overhandle a tarantula. Spiders that have been frequently handled for years without showing any resentment may bite without any detectable provocation. But you cannot *underhandle* your pet. Whenever you pick it up, you're putting it in an insecure situation; the spider would much rather have its feet planted firmly on the ground. Still, learning to handle your pet properly and without fear can prove to be quite convenient in transporting the spider and in impressing your friends.

Most tarantulas sold as pets are burrowing species and will be right at home if provided with soil into which they can dig themselves. Even if a soil base is provided for the tarantularium some sort of sheltered hideaway should be provided; here an angled rock provides shelter. Photo by Dr. Herbert R. Axelrod.

Opposite:
Gravel sprinkled on the bottom of the tarantularium provides a much less suitable substratum than soil for the spider's digging activities, so an angled rock (a piece of aquarium shale) has been provided as a refuge for the spider. The cactus and driftwood are purely decorative although most tarantularium decorations are avidly explored by the tarantula. Photos by Dr. Herbert R. Axelrod.

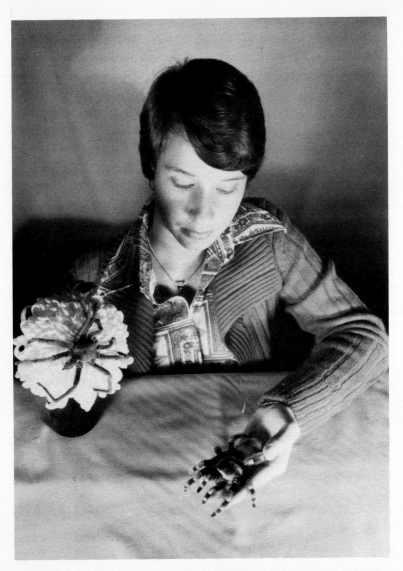

Probably the best rule to follow regarding the handling of your tarantula is: don't. Regardless of how careful you are, the potential for accidental damage still exists, and since the tarantula is totally without any need for human affection and handling, nothing is to be gained by picking it up unnecessarily. And never, never, never use your tarantula in some type of dumb show-off business by waving it around someone who might be terrified of it. Photo by Dr. Herbert R. Axelrod.

Training

I like to think that my spider is very intelligent. While she is sitting there for days it's fun to suppose she is in some deep form of contemplative meditation, taking in everything around her with the nerves in each hair and pondering the solutions to all the problems in the universe. Unfortunately, this is probably not the case.

Arachnologists do not agree on how intelligent spiders are. They conducted one experiment with an orb weaver—a small spider that ordinarily drops from its web whenever it hears a loud noise. At the sound of a tuning fork, the spider would drop, yet after nine times it no longer left its web, and by the end of two weeks it didn't even move when the fork was struck. Tarantulas have been known to leave their burrows and come to the person who makes a habit of feeding them. It is believed that this behavior results from a conditioned reflex rather than intelligence, but it does demonstrate that the spider has a memory.

You can make your pet appear as if it is obeying your commands if you study its behavior so that you know what it is going to do anyhow. The owners of flea circuses have known this secret for a long time. If your spider raises up on its hind legs when you dangle something over it, this natural act can be preceded by the command "Sit up." The more you observe your pet, the more "tricks" can come to mind. If all else fails, you can always use the command "Stay."

This Mexican tarantula is probably an *Aphonopelma* species. Photo by Dr. Sherman A. Minton.

A tarantula photographed in its natural habitat of arid semi-wasteland. Most tarantulas sold as pets inhabit desert or semi-desert habitats, although there are tarantulas that come from forested and moist areas. Photo by Dr. Sherman A. Minton.

Eurypelma californicus. Photo by Ken Lucas.

Moulting

One morning if you look into the cage and see two tarantulas instead of one, don't be alarmed. The smaller, brighter one is your pet. The larger one, which may look more like your pet after a fight, is only the discarded skin.

Tarantulas moult about four times a year for their first two years, two times a year for the next four years, and mature spiders shed their skin at least once a year. In general, males moult fewer times than females. The spider will not eat for a short time before moulting and will spin itself a carpet of silk to lie on during the shedding operation. The process usually lasts the better part of a day; during this time, if the spider is missing any appendages, the missing parts are usually regenerated.

Some time ago, my wife called me at work and through her tears she told me that our spider, Alice Brown, was lying on her back dying. I told her that Alice was beginning the moulting process and to take notes on what happened. The following, in her own words, is what she observed:

March 30, 1976

Found the spider (Alice Brown) lying on her back in the extreme corner of the case. There is no movement at all. All legs are drawn slightly inward (halfway between the ground and her body). The first and second pair of legs are toward the front part of the body, while the fourth and fifth are pointed slightly back. The chelicerae are drawn tightly shut. All of this is first observed at 8:10 a.m. of the above date.

8:40 — there has been no change.

8:56 — all of the ends of the legs wiggled quickly for about five seconds, then stopped in the first position.

9:10 — ends of the legs wiggled again (this movement is a large and rapid flexing of the legs), lasting about 2½ seconds. Then spider resumed original position.

9:13 — legs flexed up and down and then stopped after one second.

9:23 to 9:31 — unobserved.

9:31 to 9:45 — no change.

9:45 to 10:00 — unobserved. I note now an observation of much silk under the spider's body.

10:33 — moved legs and chelicerae slowly. This time the movement is not so fast and the chelicerae move alternately. The legs move up and down and slightly to the sides very slowly; even the center of the body seems to tighten and release somewhat.

10:50 — the spider has not stopped moving. Sometimes the movement is very slight and at other moments it is much more defined and active. It is now clear to see that slowly the spider is turning toward one side.

10:56 — the spider is half turned to the right and you can see the old skin wiggling and the "new" spider pulling and pushing her way out. The "old" spider's skin is brown and the "new" spider is black. The new fangs, instead of dark black, are clear. The spider is still on her back but now turned halfway over. It is a very exciting time for me to observe. The spider is slowly pushing the skin off the ends of the legs, and underneath the body is the old carapace.

11:10 — now all of the old skin has been pushed off the legs and then back off the abdomen. The spinnerets are seen at this time pushing the old skin back. Now the old skin is pushed to the side. The spider is still on her back and still moves her legs, but very slowly.

11:15 — now the spider pulls her legs close to her body and rests. She is a bright, glossy black, looking much

Aphonopelma emilia, popularly called orange-knee tarantula. Photo by Ken Lucas.

Immediately preceding a moulting, the tarantula will seek refuge to provide a sense of security while it is defenseless during the moult. Photo by Ron Daniels.

different in color than the old skin. The fangs are a translucent white.

12:00 — spider moves legs and pushes herself all the way over onto her feet.

12:30 — she has moved a few inches and is now resting in the corner of the case.

1:30 — found spider on top of old skin. She sat this way until 2:30, when she got up and pulled the skin under herself, then walked away and sat for about three minutes, then returned and sat on the skin again.

2:45 — spider starts to clean fangs and chelicerae, then lies on her side and begins cleaning her legs.

This is a very delicate operation for the tarantula. The new skin is soft, and occasionally a spider may bleed to death, although this is rare. It's best not to handle your pet for a while following the moulting process.

An unidentified Mexican tarantula. Photo by Dr. Sherman A. Minton.

Opposite:
The identification of the many species of tarantula is not easy, even for experts, and tarantula hobbyists who are interested in their animals but don't care to get involved in the fine points of taxonomic niceties will have to rely on getting familiar with the color patterns and markings and relative sizes and other obvious external features of the common species in order to be able to differentiate them. To give you an example of the type of taxonomic fine points involved, consider that the main difference between the two most common genera of native American tarantulas, *Dugesiella* and *Aphonopelma,* is that in tarantulas of the genus *Dugesiella* the hairs on the first leg joint are noticeably thick at the base, whereas in species of *Aphonopelma* the hairs are thick at the base, but not pronouncedly so. Photo by Dr. Herbert R. Axelrod.

Breeding

I know of only one person in the United States who has reared tarantulas from egg to adult—a retired college professor in Arkansas by the name of Dr. William J. Baerg. This 10-12 year experience is also open to you, if you want the challenge.

Putting two tarantulas in the same cage is risky. Even males and females may fight instead of mate; if they do mate, it's certain they will fight afterwards. This is customary with spiders: the female attempts to kill the male after the mating process. This is how the infamous black widow earned her name. If you put two spiders in the same container, have a stick ready to pry them apart if they fight.

The best time to breed the tarantula would be in the months of September and October. In his natural habitat, the male goes in search of a female at this time, soon after undergoing his last moult and producing the hooks under the knees of his front pair of legs. It is unlikely for the male to live through another autumn season with these hooks, which are necessary for the mating process, so you should be safe (or at least economical) in putting any male with these parts into the cage with your female.

Upon reaching adulthood, the male spins a small patch of silk on which he deposits a drop of seminal fluid from his genital openings, situated on the underside of his abdomen. He sucks up the fluid into the tips of his pedipalpi and is then ready to breed.

Ordinarily, when the two spiders confront each other, the male will cautiously reach out with a front leg and touch the female, whereupon she will rear up and open her fangs as if threatened. The male will then reach up and catch her fangs with his hooks and insert

The female tarantula may not fit the part of devoted mother as far as looks are concerned, but she exhibits a greater degree of parental devotion in the care of her young than many females of "higher" animal species. Photo by Muller-Schmida.

his charged pedipalpi into the female's genital openings on the underside of her abdomen. The entire mating process lasts but a few minutes. As soon as the male draws away from the female, quickly place a barrier such as a sheet of cardboard between the two spiders and remove the male from the cage.

If the breeding was successful, in a few days the female will spin a large, thick carpet of silk on which to lay approximately 500-600 tiny yellowish-green eggs. She will then gather the silk around the eggs, forming a loose egg sac averaging about an inch in diameter. This she will faithfully guard for six or seven weeks until the spiderlings hatch. Occasionally she will grasp the sac tightly with her chelicerae and move it to different places in the cage, trying to keep the eggs at the proper

An unidentified spider from Karachi, Pakistan and its intended prey. Photo by Dr. Sherman A. Minton.

An example of a jumping spider, a member of the family Salticidae. An adult jumping spider might easily be confused with a young tarantula, even though the jumping spiders and tarantulas are not closely related according to taxonomic systems now in vogue. Jumping spiders can see much better than most other spiders. Photo by Ken Lucas.

At right and below are
two spiders of the
family Araneidae
(also called
Argiopidae), the
orb-weaver spiders.
The spider at right,
Argiope aurantia, is a
common garden
spider in the United
States; the *Nephila*
species below is
found only in
southeastern portions
of the country.
Photos by
Dr. Sherman A.
Minton.

temperature. In her natural burrow the female now and then carries the sac to the entrance, where it will be warmed by the sun. Also you may find her across the cage from her sac, apparently ignoring it, yet if you were to open the cage and reach in, you would find that she is still very much on guard, as she will quickly scramble to her eggs and threaten to bite if disturbed. Be very careful not to disturb your pet at this time. If she does not attack you, she may turn and devour the egg sac.

The baby tarantulas are tiny and white, otherwise looking much like the adult. When the spiderlings hatch, they may be kept in the same cage for a few days. But soon afterwards the mother may begin to eat them, and as they grow they will start to eat each other. This is the drawback of raising tarantulas. Unless you decide to let most of the young die, you must house them individually and feed them all, and for this you would need hundreds of cages and a lot of patience. If insects cannot be found to feed all the spiderlings, the food-on-a-thread method can be used.

Besides the entertainment and feeling of accomplishment you may receive by breeding and raising tarantulas, there can be other advantages, too. For instance, the silk would make a beautiful fabric if one could get enough of it. The silkworm has been supplying mankind with silk since the 27th century B.C., yet only in laboratories have any materials been manufactured from spider silk. With today's reliance on nylon and other synthetics, the use of silk has greatly tapered off, but there are few people who do not still appreciate the art and quality of natural silk, and a scarf or blouse made from tarantula silk would be priceless. Use of spider silk as a possible substitute for DDT in killing insects is also being considered.

Another value of the tarantula may lie in its

venom. Many laboratories experiment with this fluid, and perhaps a market could be found. The venom would have to be extracted in sterile conditions for experimental purposes. To milk the venom from the spider is a fairly easy task; it can be done by means of an electric shock. This, of course, is a cruel method, and tarantulas milked this way understandably can become quite bad-tempered. A gentler method, used by Dr. Gertsch at the American Museum of Natural History, is to hook the lip of a vial under the spider's fangs and pinch the animal a little to make it "mad." The venom will run right down the glass.

The most practical and financially rewarding purpose for raising tarantulas is for selling them as pets. Pet shop owners have found that spiders sell very well. The price of a pet tarantula in the northern United States varies from $12 to $40, depending on the size and availability of the species. It is likely that a person could sell the babies as quickly as separate cages could be found for them. There is something inviting about a unique pet that would accompany its owner for up to twenty-five years and would require little care.

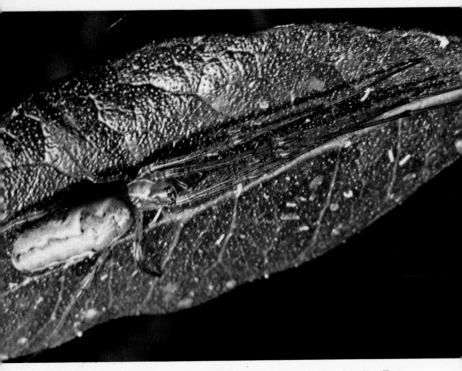

Tetragnatha species, an orb-weaving spider of the family Tetragnathidae, closely related to the orb-weaving spiders of the family Araneidae. Photo by Ken Lucas.

Two of the spider species that have at least partly accounted for the reputation of spiders as dangerous poisonous animals: Right, a black widow spider, *Latrodectus mactans* (photographed from an individual found in Perry County, Indiana); below, a brown recluse, *Loxosceles reclusa,* photographed from an individual found in Marshall County, Oklahoma. Both photos by Dr. Sherman A. Minton.

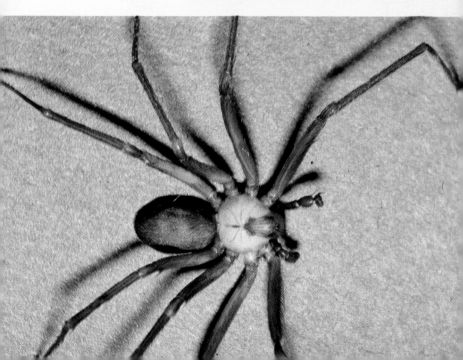

Ailments and Treatment

Tarantulas always look sick. They move so slowly that one might think they are dying; they sit for days as if dead; they refuse to eat, and so forth. The following are some "ailments" that may worry you:

If your spider refuses to eat, it is not serious. Check the temperature of the cage to see that it is kept at about 75°F—no colder than 70°F. Change its diet; see if it would like something different. But if food refusal

Although they can move fast when they want to or have to, tarantulas are generally fairly inactive, so don't worry if yours spends a lot of time lying motionless in its home. Photo by Dr. Herbert R. Axelrod.

occurs in the winter, don't worry. Many times tarantulas refuse to eat for months during the cold season because of their hibernation. Instead of digging a burrow and sleeping in it, they just don't eat. Also, the spider may not eat for awhile before moulting; this is normal. If you see remains of the spider's prey lying in the cage, this does not mean that your pet has not eaten. Often only the juices of the prey will be consumed, not the entire creature. After seizing the prey, the spider will secrete a digestive juice that changes the soft body parts of the food into a liquid which is then sucked up by the spider. Just be sure your pet has fresh water at all times, even during hibernation, and continue to offer food now and then. It will eat when it is hungry.

If your tarantula is lying on its back, looking dead, it is getting ready to shed its skin. Young ones moult four times a year; "teen-agers," twice a year; adults, once a year, usually in the spring. The spider will make a silk rug to lie on during this process. The shedding operation lasts about a day. The new skin is soft at first and has a brighter color than the old skin; it fades, in time.

Even if your spider stands motionless for days, probably nothing is wrong. This is the habit of the tarantula—a means of conserving energy. It can be frustrating, though, when you are trying to show the animal to someone and it "plays dead." Once after letting a second grade class borrow my spider for display, I received several letters from the students, one of which read:

> "Dear Dale,
> We enjoyed the tarantula. The tarantula wouldn't eat for a week. It hardly even moved its legs. It would start to after school was over.
>
> From Dale Peterson."

A crab spider (family Thomisidae) artfully camouflaged in a flower. Crab spiders don't weave webs or actively chase their food—they hide or, as here, blend artfully with their backgrounds and grab what ventures into their hiding place. Photo by Ken Lucas.

Throughout the rest of this book are illustrated a number of different animals that are more closely related to spiders than any other animals in the world; in fact, they represent different branches of the same basic group (class Arachnida) to which tarantulas and all other spiders belong. All of the non-spider arachnids shown are interesting subjects of observation, and some can be kept as pets; in addition, many are economically important in a beneficial way in that they help keep insect populations under control; some (especially the mites) are economically important for their bad effects as parasites and disease-carriers.

Above and below: vinegaroons, or whipscorpions, members of the order Uropygi. Unlike true scorpions, the tail is not equipped with a stinger, but their chelicerae can deliver a severe pinch. Shown below is the largest whipscorpion in the world, *Mastigoproctus giganteus,* native to the United States. Photo above by Dr. Sherman A. Minton; photo below by Ken Lucas.

If your spider is weak and shriveled-looking, it is thirsty. Give it some fresh water and it will revive. Many tarantulas are in this condition after traveling through the mail.

If your tarantula is female and has laid eggs and constructed an egg sac, yet had not encountered a male within the past week, the eggs are not fertilized and will not hatch. This is a rare event but it happens. She will guard the eggs faithfully as though they were fertile, but after about two months she will lose hope and devour the sac.

If your spider often appears to scratch its abdomen with its hind feet until the top of the abdomen begins to become bald, don't worry; it is not mange. Tarantulas brush off the hair of their abdomen as a form of self-defense when they feel threatened, and most of them have large bald areas on their abdomen by their next moult.

If your pet is missing a leg, don't despair. Missing appendages are regenerated during the moulting process. In the meantime, the spider is very capable of walking with what it has.

As long as a tarantula is given the proper care, there should be no true ailments to worry about. Perhaps the most critical time in the spider's health comes during the moulting process, when it is possible, although not common, for the animal to bleed to death, but this cannot be helped. The tarantula will probably be the healthiest pet you will ever own.

Conclusion

Tarantulas have been walking on this planet a lot longer than man. Perhaps even the dinosaurs knew of their bite. From the Paleozoic era to today they have changed very little—still seizing their prey and rendering themselves victims of the "tarantula hawk." As newcomers on this planet, people have been afraid of these multi-legged, furry creatures who, despite their size, boldly rear up and try to defend themselves against all odds, and we have made them subjects of shuddering tales and superstitions.

Now we are beginning to realize that these misunderstood animals have been helping us all along in the balance of nature and that they fear us as well. And we are finally learning that if we treat them with kindness they will go so far as to allow us to hold them in the palm of our hand. The frightful myths are disappearing; the old books that tell of their fatal bite are giving way to books that refer to them as timid and harmless. The movies that show them creeping over a terrified actor's chest are becoming humorous. And now this spider is seen in pet shops and in homes.

In this industrial age we are learning more and more to appreciate our environment and to live in harmony with all of Earth's inhabitants; and after 350 million years, the tarantula is finally getting the break it deserves.

Tailless whipscorpions, order Amblypygi. Above is the species *Phrynus asperatipes* (photo by Ken Lucas); below is a tailless whipscorpion of the genus *Tarantula*. Photo by Dr. Sherman A. Minton.

A windscorpion (order Solifugae). Solpugids are fast-moving, strong-jawed predators; many species are native to the United States, especially desert areas. The windscorpion shown here is eating a roach. Photo by Dr. Sherman A. Minton.

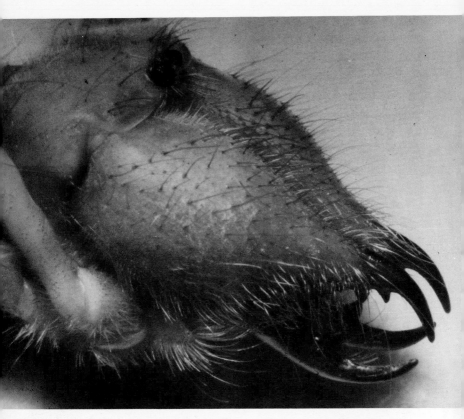

Closeup of the head of a South-West African solpugid (*Solpuga* species). Some people say that solpugids are less appealing and cute than puppies and kittens. Photo by Ken Lucas.

A male solpugid, an *Eremobates* species from Baja California.
Photo by Ken Lucas.

The solpugid species *Chanbria regalis*, from California's Anza Bor-
rego Desert. Photo by Ken Lucas.

Scorpions (order Scorpiones), which share with tarantulas a lot of bad publicity about being potentially very dangerous, have done more to earn their bad reputation. They can be dangerous from either end, and some species have been known to kill human beings. Above is an unidentified *Centruroides* species from Mexico, and below is a *Centruroides gracilis* individual found in Florida. Photos by Dr. Sherman A. Minton.

Buthotus species. Photo by Dr. Sherman A. Minton.

Parauroctonus mesaensis, an Arizona desert scorpion. Photo by Dr. Sherman A. Minton.

A female scorpion carrying her young on her back. They are ugly little things, but she likes them; scorpions are not noted for their good esthetic taste. Photo by Ken Lucas.

Hadrurus hirsutus, the giant hairy scorpion of the Mojave Desert. Photo by Ken Lucas.

A velvet mite (suborder Trombidiformes of the order Acarina). Velvet mites do not parasitize animals and in fact perform a service by eating insects and their eggs. Photo by Ken Lucas.

A ricinuleid (order Ricinulei); shown is *Cryptocellus barberi*. Ricinuleids are tiny arachnids that live among vegetative debris, eating whatever tiny prey they can catch. Photo by Ken Lucas.

This is a pseudoscorpion (order Pseudoscorpiones). Pseudoscorpions are common but, because they are small, usually go unnoticed. They live mostly among vegetative litter. Many are venomous, with poisonous glands in their pincers, but they pose no real danger to human beings. Shown is an East African species, *Titanatemnus ugandanus*. Photo by Ken Lucas.

A daddy-longlegs (order Opiliones). Most daddy-longlegs are helpful in that they destroy insect pests. The unidentified species shown is from California. Photo by Ken Lucas.

Neither the crab above (*Eriphis spinifrons*) nor the crab shown opposite are arachnids; crabs are crustaceans, related to the spiders only broadly in that they, like the spiders, are classed within the phylum Arthropoda. Taxonomically, crabs are more closely related to insects than they are to spiders.

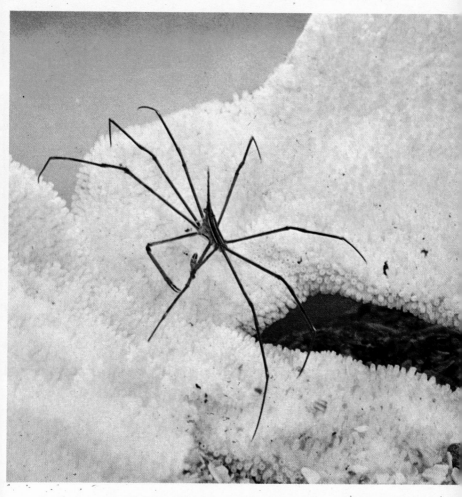

If you can have spiders that are called crab spiders because they look like or act like crabs (page 78) you can also have crabs that are called spider crabs because they look or act like spiders; the spidery-looking crab shown here is *Stenorhynchus seticornis*. Photo by Craig Barker.

Index